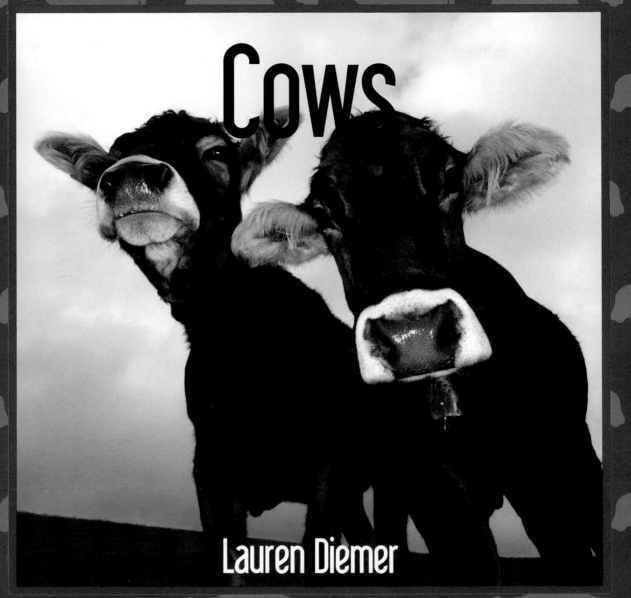

Cows

Lauren Diemer

WEIGL PUBLISHERS INC.
"Creating Inspired Learning"
www.weigl.com

Published by Weigl Publishers Inc.
350 5th Avenue, 59th Floor
New York, NY 10118
Website: www.weigl.com

Library of Congress Cataloging-in-Publication Data

Diemer, Lauren.
 Cows / Lauren Diemer.
     p. cm. -- (World of wonder. Watch them grow)
 Includes index.
 ISBN 978-1-60596-919-0 (hard cover : alk. paper) -- ISBN 978-1-60596-920-6 (soft cover : alk. paper) --
 ISBN 978-1-60596-921-3 (e-book)
 1. Cows--Juvenile literature. 2. Dairy cattle--Juvenile literature. I. Title.
 SF197.5.D54 2010
 636.2--dc22
                              2009052101

Printed in the United States of America in North Mankato, Minnesota
1 2 3 4 5 6 7 8 9 0 14 13 12 11 10

042010
WEP264000

Editor: Heather C. Hudak
Design: Terry Paulhus

All of the Internet URLs given in the book were valid at the time of publication. However, due to the dynamic nature of the Internet, some addresses may have changed, or sites may have ceased to exist since publication. While the author and publisher regret any inconvenience this may cause readers, no responsibility for any such changes can be accepted by either the author or the publisher.

Every reasonable effort has been made to trace ownership and to obtain permission to reprint copyright material. The publishers would be pleased to have any errors or omissions brought to their attention so that they may be corrected in subsequent printings.

CONTENTS

What is a Cow?

Do you know where milk comes from? It comes from a cow. Cows are large **mammals**. They live on farms in almost every part of the world. There are many types of cows. Dairy cows make the milk people drink. Beef cows are used for their meat. Draft cows pull carts and plows.

Like all animals, cows have a life cycle. They are born, grow up, and have babies of their own.

Only adult female **cattle** are called cows. Males are called bulls. Baby cattle are called calves.

Calf Season

Did you know that a cow can only make milk after she has had a baby? After a cow and a bull mate, the baby grows inside the cow. Nine months later, the calf is born. The cow will make milk for about 300 days after the calf is born.

Most cows give birth to one calf at a time. A cow will give birth to about four or five calves in her lifetime.

Calves are born wet. The cow licks the calf to clean it.

Milk Run

How much did you weigh at birth? Calves weigh 80 to 100 pounds (36 to 45 kilograms). This is about the same as a 10-to-12-year-old child.

Calves drink milk from their mother soon after they are born. The milk is stored in a **sac** called an udder. It hangs from the cow's stomach.

The first milk that cows feed their calves is not the same as milk sold in stores. It has special **vitamins** the calf needs to grow strong. After the first milk, the calf drinks regular milk from the udder.

Milk Money

How much milk do you drink in a day? A cow can make more than 90 glasses of milk each day. Calves only drink some of the milk their mothers make. The farmer collects the rest and sells it for people to drink.

Calves stop drinking milk at about six months of age. A cow will keep making milk for a few months after this. She then takes a rest from milking. This happens about three months before her next calf is born.

A New Home

How long do you plan to live with your parents? On some farms, calves stay with their mothers for just a few hours. After that, the farmer takes them to a special pen.

Many calves are born at about the same time to different cows. Sometimes, these calves are kept in the same pen. They are fed milk through bottles or **troughs** until they are six to eight weeks old. The calves then join the other cattle in the fields. There, they eat grass and **feed**.

A six-week-old calf will drink about 1 gallon (4 liters) of water each day.

Baby Weight

How much did you weigh at six months of age? Most human babies weigh about 13 to 21 pounds (5.9 to 9.5 kg) at this age. Six-month-old calves weigh about 400 pounds (181.4 kg).

When a calf reaches a certain age, it is known by another name. A heifer is a young female cow that has not had a baby. A young male is called a steer.

Growing Up

How old were your parents when you were born? Cows can begin having babies at about two years of age. At this age, cows are not yet full grown. Their size depends on the type of cow. Most weigh about 700 to 1,500 pounds (317.5 to 680 kg).

Cows stop growing when they are about four years old. At this age, they weigh about 900 to 1,800 pounds (408 to 817 kg).

In nature, cows can live up to 25 years. Most dairy cows live for about seven years.

Cow Cud

How much can you eat in a day? Cows spend about eight hours eating each day. They eat 80 to 90 pounds (36 to 41 kg) of grass, hay, barley, and corn. This is the same as eating 360 cheeseburgers.

Cows have four parts to their stomach. This helps them **digest** tough plant matter. Food moves through the first two parts of the stomach. Then, cows bring the food back up inside their mouth. This food is now called cud. Cud is chewed and swallowed. Then, it moves through the third and fourth parts of the stomach.

Cows Everywhere

Can you imagine living in a place where there are more cows than people? This is true in nine states. They are Montana, North Dakota, Idaho, Iowa, Kansas, Wyoming, South Dakota, Oklahoma, and Nebraska.

Cows are important in other parts of the world as well. Many people from India follow the Hindu faith. To them, cows are a **symbol** of life. Hindus do not eat cow meat. Many **rural** Indian families have one or more dairy cows.

Milking Cows

construction
paper

rubber glove

safety pin

tape

scissors

markers or
crayons

cup

water

1. Draw a picture of a cow on the construction paper.

2. Decorate the cow using the markers or crayons.

3. Cut out the cow shape.

4. Fill the glove half full with water.

5. Use tape to attach the glove to the cow. This will be the udder.

6. Tape the drawing to a wall.

7. Use the safety pin to poke holes in the fingers of the rubber glove.

8. Hold the plastic cup under the glove. Then, gently pull the fingers to make water pour into the cup.

Find Out More

To learn more about cows, visit these websites.

Life Cycle of a Cow
www.parmalat.com.au/information/information.cfm?/
section/3/subsection/27

All About Cows for Kids
www.kiddyhouse.com/
Farm/Cows

Just for Kids
www.braums.com/
JustKids/AllAboutCows.asp

MooMilk
www.moomilk.com

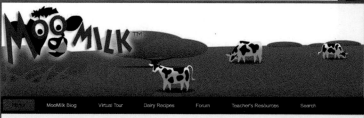

Glossary

cattle: domesticated animals belonging to the same group; includes cows, bulls, steers, or oxen

digest: the action of the stomach to break down food that is eaten

feed: a mixture of foods that cattle eat

mammals: warm-blooded animals with fur or hair that are born live and drink milk from their mother

rural: in the countryside

sac: a baglike part of the body that often contains fluid

symbol: a thing that stands for something else

troughs: a long container farmers use to feed and water animals

vitamins: substances that help the body stay healthy

Index